HISTORY

SERIES TITLES

Menchi pp. 42–43; Antonella Pastorelli pp. 20–21, 24–25, 38–39; Claudia Saraceni pp. 18–19, 34–35; Sergio pp. 14–15, 40
Smaller Illustrations: Studio Stalio (Alessandro Cantucci, Fabiano Fabbrucci, Margherita Salvadori)
Maps: Paola Baldanzi
Photos: Corbis/Contrasto, Milan pp. 17t, 30–31b, 45b
Art Director: Marco Nardi
Layouts: Rebecca Milner
Project Editor: Loredana Agosta
Research: Valerie Meek, Claire Moore
Repro: Litocolor, Florence

Consultants:
Dr. DOMINIQUE COLLON and Dr. IRVING L. FINKEL, Assistant Keepers, Department of the Ancient Near East, The British Museum

Library of Congress Cataloging-in-Publication Data

Morris, Neil, 1946-
  Mesopotamia and the Bible lands / Neil Morris.
      p. cm. -- (History of the world)
  Includes index.
  Summary: "A detailed overview of history in Mesopotamia including the various civilizations that lived there, from the Sumerians up to the founding of Christianity"--Provided by publisher.
  ISBN 978-8860981578
  1. Iraq--History--To 634--Juvenile literature. 2. Middle East--History--To 622--Juvenile literature. I. Title.
  DS71.M77 2009
  935--dc22
                                    2008008400

Printed and bound in Malaysia

MESOPOTAMIA AND THE BIBLE LANDS
was created and produced by McRae Books Srl
Via del Salviatino, 1 — 50016 — Fiesole (Florence), (Italy)
info@mcraebooks.com
www.mcraebooks.com

Publishers: Anne McRae, Marco Nardi
Series Editor: Anne McRae
Author: Neil Morris
Main Illustrations: Giacinto Gaudenzi p. 29;
MM comunicazione (Manuela Cappon, Monica Favilli) pp. 6–7, 8–9, 10–11, 13, 27, 32–33, 36–37; Alessandro

HISTORY

Mesopotamia and the Bible Lands

Neil Morris

Zak
BOOKS

Contents

Jewelry in the form of gold beads from ancient Arabia. Archeologists have found evidence of gold mines and workshops in Yemen.

Note—This book shows dates as related to the conventional beginning of our era, or the year 1, understood as the year of the birth of Jesus Christ. All events dating before this year are listed as BCE (Before Current Era). Events dating after the year 1 are defined as CE (Current Era).

TIMELINE

	8000 BCE	4500 BCE	3500 BCE	1500 BCE
 EARLY MESOPOTAMIA AND THE SUMERIANS	First farmers in Mesopotamia. Hassuna culture and Samarra culture.	Farming villages develop into small towns; the earliest plows are used.	Development of the first cities in southern Mesopotamia.	The Akkad region, north of Sumer, is supreme. Third Dynasty of Ur, the city is capital of an important empire.
 BABYLONIANS				Elamites sack Ur and capture the city's king. King Hammurabi rules Babylon.
 HITTITES			The Hittites arrive in Anatolia / Battle of Qadesh between the Hittites and Egyptians. / Fall of the Hittite Empire.	
 ASSYRIANS			The city of Ashur is settled. Hittites invade and sack Babylon. Assyrian trading colonies are founded in Antolia.	
 PHOENICIANS				Phoenician city-states start to form a major trading empire.
 PERSIANS				
ARABIAN NOMADS				
 ISRAELITES			Abraham leads his people to Canaan. Hebrews migrate from Canaan to Egypt. Judges lead Israelites.	

4

Introduction

I t was in Mesopotamia—the land between and around the Euphrates and Tigris rivers—that farmers first started growing their own crops. Their simple settlements grew into the world's first cities, leading to many interrelated cultures, kingdoms, and empires. The story of the region comprises the history of many peoples, including the Sumerians, Babylonians, Hittites, Assyrians, Phoenicians, and Persians. Together they were responsible for many amazing inventions, from the wheel to the written word. According to the Bible, Abraham's origins also lay in Mesopotamia, and we follow his migration to Canaan, the founding of the kingdom of Israel, and the years of exile and foreign occupation. Our look at many thousands of years of this fascinating region's history ends with the birth of Christianity.

Silver statuette of a fertility goddess from Anatolia.

1000 BCE	800 BCE	600 BCE	400 BCE	200 BCE

Nabopolassar, first of the Chaldean dynasty, comes to rule Babylonia.

Nebuchadnezzar II rebuilds Babylon.

Babylon is captured by Cyrus II of Persia.

Nimrud is capital.

Assyrians occupy Babylon.

Babylon is sacked after rebelling against Assyria.

Nineveh is sacked by the Babylonians and Medes.

The first Phoenician colony is founded in Cyprus.

Colonists from Tyre found the city of Carthage.

Tyre allies itself with Egypt against Assyria.

Tyre is besieged by the Babylonians.

Tyre and other cities fall under Persian rule.

Tyre is captured by Alexander the Great after an eight-month siege.

Carthage is destroyed by the Romans.

Persian ruler Hakhamanish founds the Achaemenid dynasty.

Cyrus the Great becomes king of the Medes and Persians and rules Babylon.

Cambyses II conquers Egypt.

The Persians are defeated by the Athenians.

The Persians are defeated by Alexander the Great.

Traders travel the "Incense Road."

According to legend, the Queen of Sheba visits King Solomon in Jerusalem.

Rise of states in southern Arabia.

Minaeans trade successfully from Ma'in, southern Arabia.

The Nabataeans fight off an attack by Demetrius I Poliorcetes, king of Macedonia, at their capital city of Petra.

King David makes Jerusalem capital of Israel.

Reign of Solomon.

The kingdom is divided.

The Assyrians conquer Israel.

Judah is overrun by the Babylonians; Judaeans are exiled to Babylon.

Exiled people return to their homeland.

Macedonian king rules Palestine.

Revolt of the Macabees.

Roman rule.

Life Near the Rivers
Some time after 7000 BCE, the people of Mesopotamia began digging irrigation canals from the two rivers to water their fields. They also built dykes and embankments, as well as water-storage basins, so that they could use the rivers' water throughout the year. The system of canals, especially to the east of the Euphrates, was quite large by about 4000 BCE.

Mesopotamia: The Two Rivers

Mesopotamia is the name of an ancient region where the world's first civilization developed. The region stretched from the Taurus Mountains of present-day Turkey in the north to the Persian Gulf in the south, covering parts of present-day Syria and most of Iraq. It was called Mesopotamia, meaning "land between the rivers," by the ancient Greeks. They were referring to the two great rivers that flow through the region—the Euphrates and the Tigris. They made a fertile flood plain in the south, although the summers were long and hot with little rainfall. Early farmers had to learn to use their water wisely.

The two rivers were also used for transport. Boats carried food and building materials, especially downstream towards the south (upstream was more difficult).

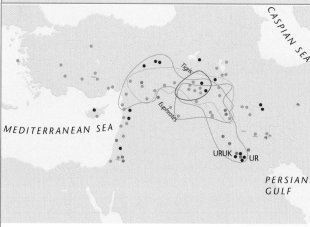

MESOPOTAMIA

CASPIAN SEA

Tigris

Euphrates

MEDITERRANEAN SEA

URUK • UR

PERSIAN GULF

— Hassuna culture 6500–6000 BCE
— Samarran culture 6000–5500 BCE
— Halafian culture 6000–5400 BCE
— Ubaid culture 5900–4300 BCE
 Evidence of irrigation c. 6000 BCE

● Settlement established before 6000 BCE
● Settlement established 6000–5400 BCE
● Settlement established 5400–4300 BCE
▪ Early pottery kilns

The Euphrates and the Tigris Rivers
The two rivers begin close to each other, high in the mountains of present-day eastern Turkey. They flow in a south-easterly direction, through modern northern Syria and Iraq to the Persian Gulf. In ancient times, the rivers flooded the Mesopotamian plains every year during spring and early summer. The floods were so strong that early farmers had to build embankments to protect their crops.

Some early Mesopotamian boats were made of bundles of reeds tied together. Other boats were made from wooden planks while rafts were kept afloat with inflated animal skins. Reed houses were built, similar to those still used in the southern marshes.

The first plows were simple wooden devices. By 3000 BCE bronze blades had been added, and some plows had funnels for dropping seeds into the ground.

Goats were herded by early farmers, along with sheep. Pigs and cattle were domesticated later. These animals were kept for their milk, hides, and wool, as well as for meat.

Clay tablets such as this one, which dates from around 3000 BCE, were used by early traders to keep account of goods. The picture symbols represent the goods, and the deeper impressions show quantities.

Farming

About 10,000 years ago, groups of hunter-gatherers who settled in Mesopotamia began growing their own crops. They started by collecting the seeds of wild grains, such as einkorn and emmer wheat. Then they planted the seeds near the river and kept the growing plants well watered. Farming villages gradually grew up near the fields of crops.

Fragment of a pitcher, made about 5200 BCE, with a face painted on its neck. Early paint was usually made from iron oxide and other minerals.

Pottery

Settled villagers found that clay pots were ideal to use as storage containers and cooking vessels. Pots were shaped by hand and then fired in a simple kiln. They were painted in a variety of designs. By about 4000 BCE, potters were using a simple turntable that they rotated by hand. A more sophisticated potter's wheel was developed later.

Bronze head of King Sargon (c. 2340–2284 BCE), who took over the city of Kish and then built a great empire, which he ruled from his capital of Akkad.

Sumer: Cities, Kings and Gods

Cities developed in a region of southern Mesopotamia that we call Sumer (from the name of the region in the Akkadian language). The Sumerians themselves called the region Kalam, meaning "the Land." They lived in cities that were surrounded by small settlements and farmland. City-dwellers lived in mud-brick houses, and in time some became craftworkers and traders. Some cities took over the nearby area, becoming city-states, and then some even conquered their neighbors as their kingdoms grew. Each city was dedicated to a god and led by a king, who was thought to have been chosen by the gods.

This bronze bull, inlaid with silver, was made some time after 2500 BCE. Bulls were seen as a symbol of strength and may have been used in religious sacrifices.

Early Cities

As the farming population grew, small settlements became towns and cities. Successful harvests and storing of food meant that some people had time to do other things, such as make jewelry or build temples. In order to control irrigation and organize people, a hierarchy grew up and led to the rule of kings. For defence against others, cities were walled. They were each dominated by a temple, which served as a house on Earth for the city's individual god.

In about 2100 BCE Ur-Nammu, a governor of the city of Ur who later became king, built a ziggurat dedicated to the moon-god Nanna. Forced donations of grain and other food to the temple's priests were carefully recorded by scribes on clay tablets.

Wooden board game dating from about 2500 BCE, found in the royal cemetery at Ur. The game probably involved moving around the board according to the throw of dice or dice-sticks.

A necklace made of beaten gold, c. 1800 BCE. The gold was probably obtained from eastern Anatolia (modern-day Turkey) or the Persian Gulf.

Trade

Early Sumerian cities exchanged goods with each other. Materials that could not be found in Mesopotamia were imported from elsewhere. From the earliest times, volcanic glass called obsidian—used to make cutting blades—was obtained from the mountains of the north and east. Before 3000 BCE the Sumerians traded with Egypt and from c. 2300 BCE with the cities of the Indus Valley. They created a network of trading routes.

Gods and Goddesses

The Sumerians worshiped many different gods and goddesses, and each city had its own special deity. One of the most important gods was Enlil, who was known as the supreme lord, father and creator. He was the brother of the mother goddess Aruru and husband to Ninlil. The Sumerians believed that it was important to perform the correct rituals when worshiping the gods, so that they would continue to favor their city.

Statue of a priestess wearing a ceremonial cloak dating from about 2400 BCE. Many priestesses served and worshiped goddesses.

Akkadian cylinder seal from about 2250 BCE. In the center, the sun god, Shamash, rises from the eastern mountains. To the right, the water god, Ea, surrounded by gushing water and fish, is attended by another god. To the left are the winged goddess of love and war, Ishtar, and a warrior-god.

Myths and Legends

Important Sumerian kings were treated as gods, and after their death legends were told of their great exploits. There were also creation myths and stories about the gods, which at the time were probably seen as historical truth. Fortunately for us, some of these were written down on clay tablets. Stories in *The Epic of Gilgamesh*, found on 12 tablets in the library of an Assyrian king, tell of how Gilgamesh showed great strength and bravery, but failed to find immortality. Only his fame lives on.

Knowledge and Invention

Some of the most important inventions in human history came from Mesopotamia. Most importantly, the Sumerians began recorded history by developing their own written language. This has helped modern historians understand more about ancient knowledge. Other developments, such as the invention of the wheel and the smelting and use of various metals, were to have a great effect well beyond the region of Mesopotamia.

The invention of wheeled carts also facilitated trade. Grain, which was traded for other valuable goods, was stored in granaries like the ones shown here in the distance.

The first wheeled carts, pulled by asses or oxen, were simple four-wheeled vehicles. Although cross-country trade routes were well known and well worn, for larger cargoes it was still often more practical to use the two great rivers. This cart with its eight-spoked wheels dates to about 650 BCE.

The Wheel

The first wheels were probably turntables made by potters, who used them to turn the clay around as they built up and shaped their pots. Around 3250 BCE, the first wheeled vehicles came into use. Early solid wheels were made of pieces of wood, cut to form a disk shape and fastened together with wooden or copper brackets. Wheeled carts were first used to transport goods, replacing earlier sledges.

The Sumerian King List was written in about 1820 BCE, making it one of the world's earliest historical records. The clay block lists kings of various Sumerian cities in chronological order.

Writing

The first Mesopotamian writing system probably developed from the use of clay tokens by early Sumerian traders. By 3500 BCE the tokens were being enclosed in clay balls, and a few hundred years later, the Sumerians were writing on flat clay tablets with pointed reed pens. The original picture signs were simplified into symbols that made up a script called cuneiform, which means "wedge-shaped." Scribes used a wedge-shaped stylus to write quickly on wet clay.

TECHNOLOGY

c. 5500 BCE
Fine painted pottery of the Halaf culture in northern Mesopotamia.

c. 4500 BCE
First use of sail on Mesopotamian rivers.

c. 3500 BCE
First turntables used by Mesopotamian potters; copper is used.

c. 3400 BCE
Temple officials in Sumer replace stamps with cylinder seals that can be rolled over soft clay to make a continuous design.

c. 3250 BCE
Pictographic writing on clay tablets.

c. 3000 BCE
First cuneiform inscriptions.

c. 2600 BCE
The use of bronze is developed.

c. 2100 BCE
The first ziggurats are built in Sumerian cities; "fast" potter's wheel is already in use to throw pottery.

c. 2000 BCE
Spoked wheels are introduced; shortly afterwards, horse-drawn two-wheeled chariots are developed for military use; bronze is widely used.

Metalwork

Copper and bronze (an alloy of copper and tin), and later iron, were the metals most used in ancient Mesopotamia. The metals were extracted from their ores by smelting. This involved burning wood, reeds, and charcoal in a furnace and using bellows to fan the fire and raise the temperature. The metal could then be removed and later re-melted to pour into molds. Gold and other metals could also be hammered into shape.

Long daggers such as this were common around 1500 BCE, often cast as one piece in bronze.

This ceremonial gold helmet was made in Ur about 2500 BCE. The small holes around the edges meant that leather padding could be attached to the helmet.

This beautiful Sumerian lyre was made around 2500 BCE. The bull's head is made of gold, and its eyes are of lapis lazuli. Music played an important part in religious rites, royal ceremonies, and public festivals. Harps, pipes and percussion instruments were also common.

Early Babylonia: Rule of Law

Around 4,000 years ago the city of Ur lost its power in Mesopotamia. Other cities, such as Isin and Larsa, fought for supremacy, but it was Babylon that eventually came to rule over the whole region. The city's name came from an Akkadian word meaning "gateway of the god." It lay on the Euphrates, to the north of the other cities. Babylon had a dynasty of kings that grew in power, and they ruled for centuries over a region that came to be known as Babylonia. Historians call the four centuries between 2000 and 1600 BCE the Old Babylonian period. The greatest Babylonian ruler was Hammurabi, who introduced a system of laws throughout his kingdom.

Laying Down the Law

Hammurabi established a famous Code of Laws, which was made up of at least 280 "cases of justice." The laws were written on clay tablets and sent around Babylonia to serve as models of behavior. Though many of the suggested punishments were harsh, the king saw it as his duty to "protect the orphan and widow." Two of the laws read: "If a man has put out the eye of a free man, they shall put out his eye. … If a slave has struck the cheek of a free man, they shall cut off his ear."

This stele lists Hammurabi's laws. It was found at Susa, in Elam, where it had been taken as war booty. The carving on top shows the king standing before Shamash, the sun god and patron of justice.

Kingdom of Babylon

Babylon, on the east bank of the Euphrates, was an unimportant town until about 1894 BCE. Then it was taken over by the first of a line of rulers from an Amorite tribe, a wandering people from Mesopotamia. Babylon was still quite a small kingdom when Hammurabi came to the throne, but by the end of his reign it controlled the whole of Mesopotamia.

Stone head of King Hammurabi. He undertook great building works in Babylon, as well as improving the defence of his kingdom and the irrigation of its lands.

Expanding Trade

In years of good harvests Babylonia had enough grain for merchants to export and exchange for timber, stone, and other goods. If there was no direct exchange, payment was usually in silver. Ur was still an important trading city, with boats coming up from the Persian Gulf, and it had its own merchants' organization. Some traders also acted as royal envoys, carrying valuable gifts between rulers.

This relief, dating to about 700 BCE, shows a merchant leading a camel loaded with goods. Camels were well suited to the harsh conditions of desert trade routes.

EARLY MESOPOTAMIAN TRADE ROUTES

Babylonian Trade

Babylonia lay on the main trade routes between the Persian Gulf and the Mediterranean Sea. One of the main stops on the Euphrates to the north of Babylon was the city of Mari, which was known for its tin trade. Mari was finally conquered by Hammurabi.

MEDITERRANEAN SEA

Tigris

MARI

BABLYON

NIPPUR

Euphrates

KISH

LARSA

LAGASH

URUK

UR

Babylonian Empire of Hammurabi c. 1792–1750 BCE

Trade routes

Looking to the Heavens

The Babylonians greatly increased their knowledge of astronomy by keeping detailed records of their observations of the stars and planets. They likened the wandering planets to wild goats and the fixed stars to tame goats. Their greatest purpose in looking at the night sky was to predict future events. The Babylonians believed that what happened up in the heavens was mirrored down on Earth.

Astronomers study an eclipse of the Sun, which was generally seen as an omen of disaster. A scribe carefully records their findings.

A carving showing the sun god Shamash on his throne receiving a king and two other gods. The disk in the center symbolizes the Sun.

Sacred Sacrifice

Religious festivals were important in Babylonia, and many involved great processions. These gave ordinary people the opportunity to take part in religious events and communicate with the gods. There were festivals of thanksgiving, and many were associated with the phases of the Moon. Special events took place at New Year, which was celebrated in spring, at the beginning of the month of Nisannu (around mid-March by our calendar). During some sacred festivals, a bull was led outside the city before being sacrificed.

Statue of a goddess that acted as a fountain in the courtyard of the palace at Mari.

A king leads the procession of a bull sacrifice.

The Babylonian Way of Life

The Babylonians lived in a similar way to earlier peoples of Mesopotamia. They had mud-brick houses, and their successful farming methods meant that food was good and plentiful. Grains such as barley were ground into flour and used to make bread, beer, and porridge-like soups. Vegetables were grown, and fish, sheep, and goats were also eaten. The people's rulers and priests organized seasonal festivals, and everyone worshiped Marduk, the patron god of Babylon from early times. But after their great king Hammurabi died in about 1750 BCE, the Old Babylonian Empire gradually went into decline.

Interpreting Omens

The Babylonians believed that the gods sometimes allowed them to see into the future by interpreting omens. Diviners were specialists at prediction. They often examined the entrails of slaughtered animals, looking especially at the liver for any peculiarities. They sometimes poured drops of oil into a beaker of water and studied the shapes made, or they watched clouds of smoke rising from burning incense. In this way they gained insight into the will of the gods.

Clay model of a sheep's liver. The shape of the real liver was examined and omens written on the model. This one ominously forecasts the destruction of small towns.

This terra-cotta plaque showing a loving couple, dating from about 1900–1600 BCE, was found at Ur.

Marriage

By the laws of Hammurabi, a wife received a written contract of marriage from her husband. Men generally had only one wife, and her main duty was to produce children, especially sons. If she failed to do this, her husband could divorce her, but he had to return any money paid to him when they married. She also had the right to a divorce if her husband disgraced her and she could show that she was blameless. According to the law, a man could leave his property to his wife rather than to his sons.

Women's Roles

Wives and especially mothers of kings had great power and authority. Women could also be scribes in royal palaces. Priestesses had special roles, and some were allowed to buy and sell fields. Among ordinary people, both weaving and the brewing of beer were normally done by women, and each activity had its own goddess—Uttu for weaving and Ninkasi for beer-making.

This terra-cotta statue of a woman, dating about 2000–1700 BCE, was probably placed in a temple.

HITTITES

c. 2300 BCE
The Hittites arrive in Anatolia, probably from the central Asian region.

c. 1700–1400 BCE
Period of the Hittite Old Kingdom.

c. 1650 BCE
Hattusa is made capital of the Hittite kingdom.

c. 1595 BCE
Mursilis I (reigned c.1620–1590 BCE) invades and sacks Babylon.

c. 1550 BCE
The kingdom of Mitanni is founded.

c. 1400–1190 BCE
Period of the Hittite New Kingdom (or Hittite Empire).

c. 1370–1330 BCE
Reign of Suppililiumas I, one of the greatest Hittite kings.

1350 BCE
The Hittites destroy the kingdom of Mitanni.

c. 1340 BCE
The Hittites conquer western Mitanni.

c. 1275 BCE
Battle of Qadesh between the Hittites and Egyptians.

c. 1190 BCE
Fall of the Hittite Empire as Hattusa is destroyed.

Masters of Metal

The Hittites were great metalworkers, skilled at making objects in gold, silver, and other metals. They were probably the first people to smelt iron, and so helped bring in the true Iron Age. Certainly iron was in use as early as 2000 BCE in Anatolia, when it may have been considered more valuable than gold. By 1400 BCE it had become a very important metal, and the Hittites found it useful for making strong, dependable weapons.

Gold pendant figurine of a god wearing a typical Hittite conical hat, from about 1300 BCE.

The guardian warrior-god of the King's Gate at Hattusa is armed with a battleaxe and a curved dagger.

Rise of the Hittites

The Hittites invaded Anatolia, to the northwest of Mesopotamia in present-day Turkey, around 2000 BCE. They built a kingdom, and about 400 years later the Hittite king went down the Euphrates to Babylon and defeated its Amorite ruler. The Hittites soon returned to their own capital of Hattusa, leaving a new dynasty of Kassite kings from the east to rule Babylon. The Hittites were a warrior people, and from 1400 BCE they built an empire by taking over Mesopotamian cities and small states. These territories were then ruled by locals under the authority of the Hittite king.

Horsemen

Throughout ancient Mesopotamia the horse was known as the "donkey of the mountains." The Hittites became expert at breeding and training horses, mainly for pulling their war chariots (see page 18). Horses were also used by kings, princes, and important landowners.

Decorative part of a bronze standard, in the shape of a man and his horse, from Anatolia, about 2000 BCE.

THE HITTITE EMPIRE

TROY
ALACA
HATTUSA
YAZILIKAYA
SMYRNA
KANESH
MALATYA
MILETUS
MERSIN
CARCHEMISH
ALEPPO
UGARIT
HAMATH
QADESH
MEDITERRANEAN SEA

■ Hittite heartland
□ Hittite area of influence

The Hittite Capital

In the middle of the 17th century BCE, the Hittite King Labarnas (reigned c. 1650–1620 BCE) made Hattusa, in Anatolia, his capital and took the name Hattusilis ("the one from Hattusa"). A later Hittite king fortified the city, rebuilding the walls around the original citadel and the whole city. A royal palace and several temples were added. In the southern section of the city there were three large gates in the double walls: one was flanked by guardian stone lions, another by sphinxes, and a third by a warrior-god.

Hittite Culture

After the fall of the Hittite Empire, some city-states survived in south-eastern Turkey and northern Syria under their own dynasties. Arameans also established principalities alongside the Neo-Hittite ones. They adopted aspects of Hittite culture, particularly in architecture and the way they decorated their buildings with relief sculpture, guardian sphinxes, and lions. As a result, Neo-Hittite culture survived until these small kingdoms were taken over by Assyria in 710 BCE.

Detail of a stone relief showing scenes of everyday life of a Neo-Hittite king of Carchemish (northern Syria) and his family. Here two young princes play a game of knucklebones.

Range of Gods

The Hittites believed in many different gods and goddesses. As their empire grew, they adopted the gods of the people they conquered, so the range became even larger. One of the main Hittite deities was the storm-god of Hatti who was often shown carrying a trident or a bolt of lightning as he drove his chariot drawn by two sacred bulls. Teshup was the companion of the sun-goddess Arinna.

This pitcher from about 1550 BCE was used for pouring wine, oil, or honey for the gods.

A golden disk surrounds the head of the protective sun-goddess Arinna, who was seen as the queen of heaven. The Hittite king and queen were her high priest and priestess.

Fragments of a Hittite clay tablet outlining the peace treaty. It says that the treaty was also inscribed on a silver tablet that was sent to Egypt, but this has never been found.

A Clash of Empires

As the Hittites moved south along trade routes beside the Syrian Desert, they clashed with the Egyptian Empire as it spread north from Africa. The meetings of the two empires were not always hostile. In the 14th century BCE the widow of an Egyptian pharaoh asked the Hittite king to send one of his sons to become her husband. But the young king was killed before this could happen. Then, around 1275 BCE, Hittite king Muwatallis II fought the Egyptian pharaoh Ramesses II at Qadesh, in modern Syria. Less than a century later, the Hittite Empire and its capital were destroyed, probably by the Kashka people from the Black Sea area.

Battle of Qadesh

The great battle began when Ramesses II (reigned 1279–1213 BCE) fell into a trap. He believed false reports that the Hittite army was still further north, at Aleppo. When the Hittites forded the Orontes River and suddenly attacked, the Egyptians were unprepared. Their first division was destroyed, but they fought back with the help of an auxiliary force. After two days the battle ended in stalemate, and the Egyptians moved back to the south. Later, both sides claimed a great victory.

War Chariots

The Hittite chariot was much lighter and faster than earlier Mesopotamian models. It was pulled by two specially trained horses, and the army kept other horses in reserve as replacements. The wooden chariot was wide enough to carry three men. The driver stood in the middle, and he was flanked on one side by an attacking spearman and on the other side by a defensive shield-bearer.

The Peace Treaty

Sixteen years after the Battle of Qadesh, Muwatallis's brother Hattusilis III (reigned 1275–1245 BCE) signed a historic peace treaty with Ramesses II. The two rulers agreed not to attack each other and to help the other if there were a threat from elsewhere, such as Assyria. The treaty was further sealed in 1246 BCE, when Hattusilis sent his eldest daughter to become a wife to Ramesses II.

With its spoked wheels and its axle set well back, the Hittite chariot was balanced and highly maneuverable.

During the battle, the Hittites and the Egyptians used similar weapons. Both sides had many thousands of foot soldiers and charioteers. Ramesses II's four divisions contained 5,000 men each, but the Hittite army might still have outnumbered them. Both armies suffered great casualties.

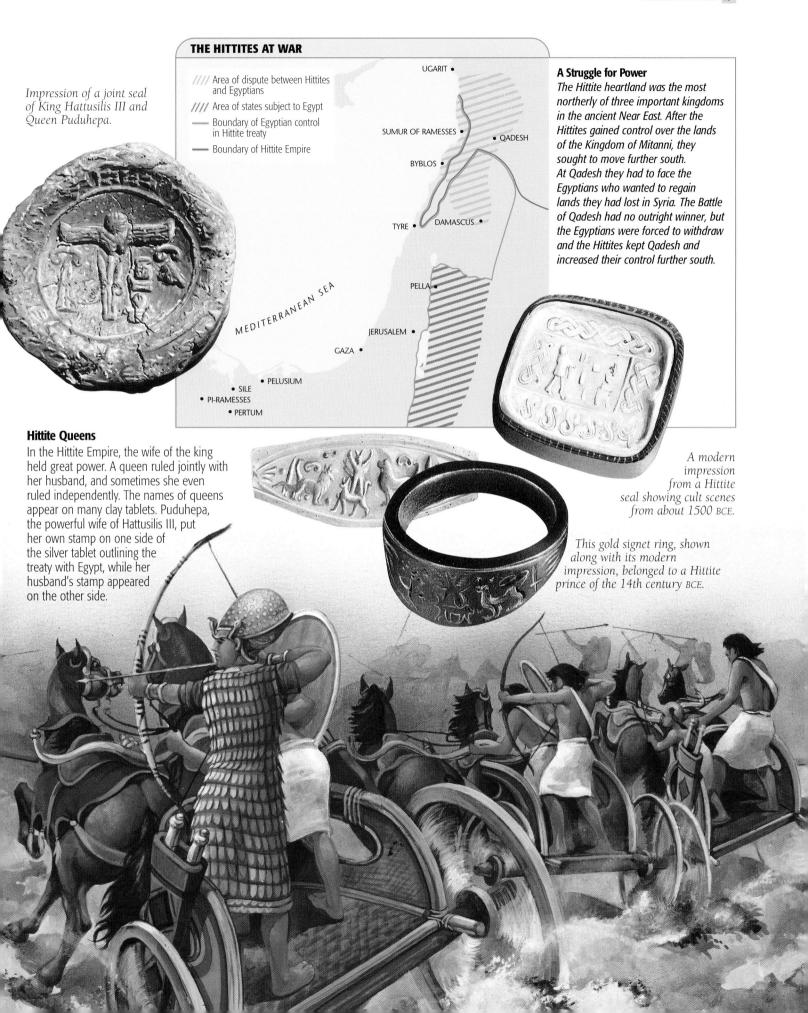

Impression of a joint seal of King Hattusilis III and Queen Puduhepa.

THE HITTITES AT WAR

//// Area of dispute between Hittites and Egyptians

//// Area of states subject to Egypt

── Boundary of Egyptian control in Hittite treaty

── Boundary of Hittite Empire

UGARIT ●

SUMUR OF RAMESSES ●

QADESH ●

BYBLOS ●

TYRE ●   DAMASCUS ●

MEDITERRANEAN SEA

PELLA ●

JERUSALEM ●

GAZA ●

● PELUSIUM

● SILE
● PI-RAMESSES

● PERTUM

A Struggle for Power

The Hittite heartland was the most northerly of three important kingdoms in the ancient Near East. After the Hittites gained control over the lands of the Kingdom of Mitanni, they sought to move further south. At Qadesh they had to face the Egyptians who wanted to regain lands they had lost in Syria. The Battle of Qadesh had no outright winner, but the Egyptians were forced to withdraw and the Hittites kept Qadesh and increased their control further south.

Hittite Queens

In the Hittite Empire, the wife of the king held great power. A queen ruled jointly with her husband, and sometimes she even ruled independently. The names of queens appear on many clay tablets. Puduhepa, the powerful wife of Hattusilis III, put her own stamp on one side of the silver tablet outlining the treaty with Egypt, while her husband's stamp appeared on the other side.

A modern impression from a Hittite seal showing cult scenes from about 1500 BCE.

This gold signet ring, shown along with its modern impression, belonged to a Hittite prince of the 14th century BCE.

War Machine

The Assyrians had a powerful army. In the 8th century BCE, military reforms created an efficient war machine that included foot soldiers armed with bows and arrows, others with swords, spears, and battleaxes, as well as archers on horseback. The cavalrymen gradually replaced charioteers. The army also used wooden siege engines and heavy battering rams. Assyrian conquerors butchered and terrorised their opponents, which discouraged others from resisting them.

This Assyrian foot soldier of about 740 BCE carries a spear and a painted shield. He wears a coat of bronze or iron scale armor.

In 701 BCE King Sennacherib besieged and then destroyed the city of Lachish, in Palestine. This relief shows a family being taken into exile in Assyria.

Ashurnasirpal's Palace

Around 878 BCE King Ashurnasirpal II used workmen from conquered lands to build an enormous palace in the new capital of Nimrud, beside the Tigris. Sculptors and artists carved reliefs and painted murals on the walls of the palace, which also contained great stone statues of mythical animals. When it was finished, the king held a huge banquet and the festivities went on for ten days.

King Ashurnasirpal II receives Phoenician guests in a palace courtyard beside his throne room. The guests bring valuable gifts as tribute to the king.

The Assyrians

The homeland of the Assyrians centered on the hills and fertile plains of northern Mesopotamia, beside the River Tigris. From about the 14th century BCE, the small kingdom began to grow. The Assyrians were surrounded by many other states, and they fought their way to an empire. They became famous for their military strength and brutal treatment of their victims. They were happy with this, because their reputation made it easier for them to conquer others. Many of those they defeated were captured and made to work as slaves on huge building projects. This helped the mighty empire grow.

Gods and Demons

The chief god of Assyria was Ashur, who may originally have been the local god of the ancient city of the same name. Ninurta was the all-important god of war and had his own temple at Nimrud. Most of the Assyrian gods and goddesses were similar to those of Sumer and Babylon. The Assyrians also believed in demons and evil spirits.

An Assyrian queen's crown. Made of gold and semiprecious stones, it was beautifully worked into flowers, vines, and guardian spirits.

THE NEO-ASSYRIAN EMPIRE

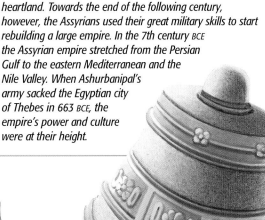

MEDITERRANEAN SEA
MESOPOTAMIA
ASSYRIA
SYRIA
BABYLONIA
EGYPT

■ Neo-Assyrian Empire 934–912 BCE
■ Neo-Assyrian Empire 883–859 BCE
■ Neo-Assyrian Empire c. 680–627 BCE

A Growing Empire

During the 11th century BCE, nomadic invaders from the north, east, and west squeezed the Assyrians back into their heartland. Towards the end of the following century, however, the Assyrians used their great military skills to start rebuilding a large empire. In the 7th century BCE the Assyrian empire stretched from the Persian Gulf to the eastern Mediterranean and the Nile Valley. When Ashurbanipal's army sacked the Egyptian city of Thebes in 663 BCE, the empire's power and culture were at their height.

THE ASSYRIANS

c. 2500 BCE
The ancient city of Ashur is settled, probably by local peoples.

c. 1950 BCE
Assyrian trading colonies are founded in Anatolia.

c. 1307–1275 BCE
Reign of King Adad-nirari, who expands Assyria's frontiers.

c. 934–911 BCE
Reign of Ashur-dan II, who re-conquers lands previously held by the Assyrians.

883–859 BCE
Reign of Ashurnasirpal II.

c. 878–707 BCE
Nimrud is capital.

744–727 BCE
Reign of Tiglath-pileser III.

729 BCE
Assyrians occupy Babylon.

721–705 BCE
Reign of Sargon II.

c. 707–705 BCE
Khorsabad is capital.

c. 704 BCE
Nineveh becomes capital under Sennacherib (reigned 704–681 BCE).

689 BCE
Babylon is sacked after rebelling against Assyria.

668–627 BCE
Reign of Ashurbanipal.

652–648 BCE
Civil war ends with Assyrian victory.

612 BCE
Nineveh is sacked by the Babylonians and Medes.

Assyrian Society

Assyria's rulers were powerful men who put great emphasis on authority and discipline. In Assyrian society, women had little say in important matters, and artists and craftsmen used their skills to portray their state's strength. Nevertheless, under King Ashurbanipal a huge library of Sumerian, Babylonian, and Assyrian clay tablets was put together at Nineveh. By then there was growing unrest among Assyria's enemies, and at the end of the 7th century BCE Nineveh fell to a group of subject states led by Babylon. This brought an end to the Assyrian Empire.

Women in Assyria

It seems that women had a lower social position and less authority than they did in Babylonia or among the Hittites. A man could send his wife away without any divorce settlement. If she committed adultery, he was allowed to beat her severely or even kill her. Outside the house, a woman had to wear a veil and observe many other restrictions. Royal women held more power, but they exercised it behind the scenes.

Smiling female face carved in ivory in the 8th century BCE.

Stone carving from about 860 BCE showing the preparation of food. Clockwise from top left: ingredients are collected from a storeroom; whisks are used to keep flies away; a baker checks his oven; butchering and carving meat.

These bracelets of gold and semiprecious stones were found in a queen's tomb beneath the palace at Nimrud.

Fashion and Style

Men and women wore long woolen tunics with narrow short sleeves. Male officials and military officers wore a shawl over the tunic. Linen was also used for clothing, and cotton was introduced around 700 BCE. The Assyrians often went barefoot, but leather sandals were sometimes worn. Both men and women wore jewelry, such as earrings and amulets. Women also had ankle bracelets.

The Royal Hunt

It was the king's duty to protect his people from danger. This included the threat from lions, which were seen as a symbol of brutal strength. Mesopotamian kings had hunted lions since the earliest times, and the Assyrians continued this tradition. In later times, the royal hunt took place in a specially enclosed park. After killing a lion, the king poured oil or wine over the dead animal and offered it to the gods.

In this carved relief, the king thrusts his spear into a leaping lion. Showing how ferocious the animals were, another lion attacks the king's spare horse.

Assyrian noblemen had square-cut beards and wore their hair long. Both hair and beard were waved and curled at the ends.

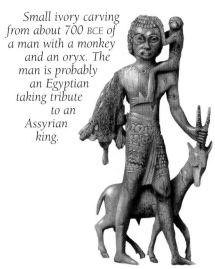

Small ivory carving from about 700 BCE of a man with a monkey and an oryx. The man is probably an Egyptian taking tribute to an Assyrian king.

Overwhelming Art

The classical style of Assyrian art was developed in the 9th century BCE, during the reign of two great conquerors, Ashurnasirpal II and his son Shalmaneser III (reigned 858–824 BCE). The forceful style was shown at its best in their capital of Nimrud, where the palaces, temples, and statues were meant to overwhelm both their own people and any potential opponents.

This statue of King Ashurnasirpal II was discovered at Nimrud.

Monumental Power

Assyrian kings took every opportunity to show their great power. Sargon II founded his own new capital at Dur-Sharrukin (modern-day Khorsabad, in Iraq). He built a monumental palace on a hill overlooking the city, and smaller temples to the main gods were put up within the grounds. This allowed Sargon II to dominate the capital and supervise the priests.

This huge stone statue of a winged bull with the head of a bearded man guarded the entrance to the throne room in the palace of Sargon II. Assyrian sculptors gave these mythical figures five legs, so that they looked natural and balanced when viewed from the side or the front.

The Last Babylonian Empire

In 626 BCE, the first of a new dynasty of kings came to rule Babylonia. The new king belonged to a people known as Chaldeans, who lived in southern Iraq and the region near the Persian Gulf. The greatest ruler of this period of the Neo-Babylonian Empire was Nebuchadnezzar II (reigned c. 605–561 BCE). He rebuilt the capital of Babylon in magnificent style, adding fortified walls, a new palace, temples and other impressive buildings. He also expanded and strengthened his empire. After Nebuchadnezzar II's death, the Empire soon began to lose power. It had lasted for less than a century when the Persians invaded and made Babylonia part of their own empire.

Terracotta figure from about 600 BCE. The animal may be a dog and represent Gula, the goddess of healing. Dogs were also thought to offer magic protection.

Historians believe that the Hanging Gardens might have been located to the west of the Ishtar Gate, between the royal palace and the Euphrates. Perhaps Nebuchadnezzar II and his homesick wife went to the uppermost level to enjoy the flowing waters and a wonderful view over the city.

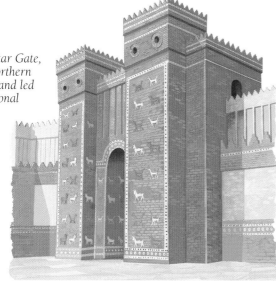

The magnificent Ishtar Gate, which formed the northern entrance to the city and led to the great Processional Way. This double gateway was covered with blue-glazed bricks and decorated with serpent-headed dragons and bulls.

Walls and Gates

The city of Babylon was protected by strong double walls, with nine gates, all named after deities. The main gate was dedicated to the Babylonian goddess of love and war, Ishtar. The walls had towers at regular intervals and were surrounded by a moat filled from the Euphrates. The walls were up to 82 feet (25 m) high and wide enough for four-horsed chariots to turn around.

The City

There was a large temple precinct dedicated to the god Marduk. It included a tall, six-level ziggurat, with a shrine to Marduk on top. This was reached by a monumental stairway, and the ziggurat included two further sets of steps. The ziggurat was about 295 feet (90 m) square. This ziggurat was probably the inspiration for the biblical Tower of Babel.

Stele depicting King Nabonidus, the last king of the Neo-Babylonian Empire, with the divine symbols of the moon-god Sin, the winged disk of the sun-god Shamash, and star of Ishtar.

This 5th-century BCE tablet is one of a series that lists the main events of Babylonian history from 747 BCE, including Nebuchadnezzar II's conquests.

Imperial Conquest

As well as rebuilding Babylon, Nebuchadnezzar II extended and strengthened the Empire. Before he became king, he marched the Babylonian army up the Euphrates to Carchemish (in modern Turkey), where he defeated the Egyptians. Then, as king, Nebuchadnezzar II secured Damascus and twice attacked Jerusalem. This led to many Judaeans being deported (see page 43).

The Phoenicians: Masters of the Sea

Phoenician Origins

The Phoenicians probably called themselves *Kenaani*, or Canaanites. They occupied the coastal strip of ancient northern Canaan that forms present-day Lebanon. They became known to the Greeks as *Phoinikoi*, from their word for "reddish purple." This probably referred to the dye for which the Phoenicians became famous.

The Phoenicians lived along a narrow coastal strip of northern Canaan. There they built important city-states, such as Byblos, Sidon, and Tyre. They were successful traders and skillful craftworkers, and above all they were adventurous seafarers. By the 8th century they had settled faraway colonies and their strong merchant ships were carrying cedar wood and oil, purple-dyed cloth, and many other goods all around the Mediterranean. After their homeland came under Assyrian control, the Phoenician settlements gained independence under the most important colony, Carthage.

This black stone coffin was made for King Eshmunazar II of Sidon (reigned 475–461 BCE), in the 5th century BCE. It bears an inscription in praise of the king and his family in Phoenician script.

Trade Goods

The Phoenicians' greatest natural resource was wood, from their forests of cedar and pine. The fertile land away from the coast also produced grapes, olives, dates, and figs. As traders, they imported linen from Egypt, grain from southern Canaan, wool from Syria, silver and iron from the western Mediterranean, semiprecious stones from Arabia, and gold and ivory from Africa.

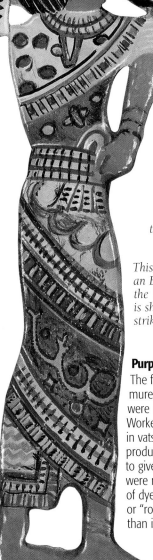

This Canaanite, from an Egyptian mosaic of the 12th century BCE, is shown wearing a striking dyed tunic.

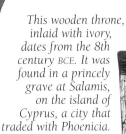

This wooden throne, inlaid with ivory, dates from the 8th century BCE. It was found in a princely grave at Salamis, on the island of Cyprus, a city that traded with Phoenicia.

This clay vessel from the 7th century BCE was probably used for carrying wine or oil. It is decorated with dancers in a sacred garden.

Carthage

After being colonised in the 8th century BCE, Carthage (meaning "New Town") soon became the most important settlement. The colonists were independent from about 600 BCE and acted as leaders of the other Phoenician settlements. Their interests in Sicily troubled first the Greeks and then the Romans. The Carthaginians fought three unsuccessful wars (called the Punic Wars) against the Romans, who eventually destroyed Carthage.

Purple Dye

The famous purple dye was obtained from murex shellfish. These spiny-shelled sea snails were collected just off the Phoenician coast. Workers smashed the shells and put the snails in vats. As they decayed, the dead creatures produced a colored liquid that was then boiled to give the dye. Many thousands of shellfish were needed to produce just a small quantity of dye, which came to be known as "Tyrian" or "royal" purple. It was worth more than its weight in gold.

Carthaginian breastplate made of gilded bronze, worn as ceremonial armor around 250 BCE.

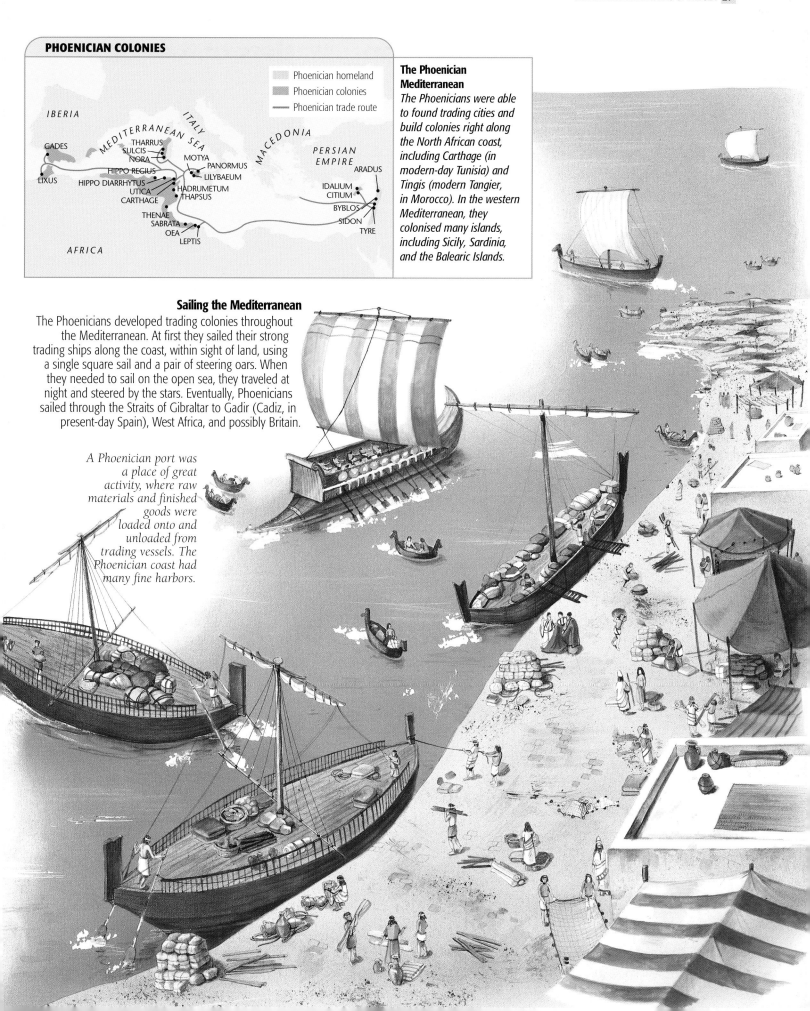

PHOENICIAN COLONIES

Legend:
- Phoenician homeland
- Phoenician colonies
- Phoenician trade route

IBERIA

MEDITERRANEAN SEA

ITALY

MACEDONIA

PERSIAN EMPIRE

AFRICA

GADES
LIXUS
THARRUS
SULCIS
NORA
HIPPO REGIUS
HIPPO DIARRHYTUS
UTICA
CARTHAGE
THENAE
SABRATA
OEA
LEPTIS
MOTYA
PANORMUS
LILYBAEUM
HADRUMETUM
THAPSUS
ARADUS
IDALIUM
CITIUM
BYBLOS
SIDON
TYRE

The Phoenician Mediterranean

The Phoenicians were able to found trading cities and build colonies right along the North African coast, including Carthage (in modern-day Tunisia) and Tingis (modern Tangier, in Morocco). In the western Mediterranean, they colonised many islands, including Sicily, Sardinia, and the Balearic Islands.

Sailing the Mediterranean

The Phoenicians developed trading colonies throughout the Mediterranean. At first they sailed their strong trading ships along the coast, within sight of land, using a single square sail and a pair of steering oars. When they needed to sail on the open sea, they traveled at night and steered by the stars. Eventually, Phoenicians sailed through the Straits of Gibraltar to Gadir (Cadiz, in present-day Spain), West Africa, and possibly Britain.

A Phoenician port was a place of great activity, where raw materials and finished goods were loaded onto and unloaded from trading vessels. The Phoenician coast had many fine harbors.

Phoenician Art and Language

The Phoenicians were known for their great skill as artists and craftsmen. They fashioned wooden furniture, often with delicate ivory inlays, and Phoenician carpenters and stone masons were even called by the king of Israel (and Judah) to help build the Temple of Jerusalem (see page 39). They excelled in making glass and working gold, silver, and bronze, combining their own Canaanite traditions with those of Mesopotamia and Egypt. The Phoenicians also developed their own alphabet, which was much simpler to learn and use than earlier writing systems. This made it easier for merchants to keep records of their extensive trading voyages around the Mediterranean.

Early Alphabet

By the 12th century BCE, or perhaps even earlier, the Phoenicians were using an alphabet to write their Semitic language. It was made up of 22 letters, or sound symbols, which were written from right to left. They were all consonants, leaving the reader to fill in the vowels. The Phoenician alphabet was adapted by the ancient Greeks, and so is the ancestor of all Western alphabets.

A Phoenician inscription on a stone tablet from Sardinia, dating to about 800 BCE.

Silver bowl decorated with human and animal figures. The Phoenicians made many shallow bowls with circular designs in gold, silver, and bronze.

Gold earrings from about 600 BCE found at the Carthaginian settlement of Tharros, in Sardinia.

Luxury Items

Phoenician artists and craftworkers were inspired by both Egyptian and Mesopotamian design traditions to make beautiful luxury items. They were especially famed for their skill with wood, metals, and carved ivory, as well as for being expert weavers and dyers. They were such successful merchants that archeologists have found Phoenician objects over a wide area, from Assyrian palaces to Sardinian towns.

Gold bracelets from Spain dating back to the 7th century BCE.

Religious Practices

Many Phoenician deities were local to individual city-states. The goddess Astarte was important at Sidon, and Melqart was the city god of Tyre. In some places, El was considered to be the father of all the gods. Earthenware urns containing the ashes of children have been found at Carthage and elsewhere. This may mean that the Phoenicians sacrificed young people to their gods.

Small marble statuette of a child, from 4th-century BCE Sidon.

Phoenician glassmakers carefully molded glass around a clay core. When the glass hardened the clay core was removed.

Glassmaking

Glass originated in Mesopotamia and Egypt, and the Phoenicians became skilled glassmakers. They learned expert techniques from the Egyptians, such as building up thin rods of semimolten glass around a clay core. They used different-colored glass to make beads and pendants for necklaces, as well as jars and other vessels. The technique of glass-blowing was probably first used in the coastal area of Phoenicia during the 1st century BCE.

THE PHOENICIANS

c. 1200 BCE
Phoenician city-states start to form a major trading empire.

c. 1000 BCE
The first Phoenician colony is founded at Kition, Cyprus.

969–936 BCE
Hiram I rules Tyre.

868 BCE
Assyrian king Ashurnasirpal II collects tribute from Phoenician cities.

c. 814 BCE
Colonists from Tyre found the city of Carthage.

701 BCE
Assyrian king Sennacherib (reigned 705–681 BCE) drives out the king of Sidon and Tyre.

c. 680 BCE
Colonies on the Balearic Islands are established.

672 BCE
Tyre allies with Egypt against Assyria.

c. 600 BCE
Carthage becomes leader of the western Phoenician colonies.

586–573 BCE
Babylonians besiege Tyre.

538 BCE
Tyre and other cities fall under Persian rule.

c. 425 BCE
Carthaginian captain Hanno (active 5th century BCE) colonises the west coast of Africa.

332 BCE
Tyre is captured by Alexander the Great after an eight-month siege.

264–241, 218–201 and 149–146 BCE
Punic Wars between Carthage and Rome.

146 BCE
Carthage is destroyed by the Romans.

PERSIA

A baked clay cylinder recording how Cyrus the Great conquered Babylon at the wish of the city's patron god, Marduk.

c. 700 BCE
Persian ruler Hakhamanish (active 7th century BCE), called Achaemenes by the Greeks, founds the Achaemenid dynasty.

c. 660–630 BCE
Reign of Cyrus I (active 7th century BCE), king of Anshan (part of ancient Elam).

550 BCE
Cyrus the Great deposes the Median king Astyages (reigned 585–550 BCE) and becomes King of the Medes and Persians.

525 BCE
Cambyses II conquers Egypt.

490 BCE
The Athenians defeat the Persians at the Battle of Marathon (in present-day Greece).

486–465 BCE
Reign of Xerxes I (son of Darius I).

480 BCE
The Persian fleet loses to the Greeks in the Bay of Salamis.

331 BCE
Alexander the Great defeats the Persian army of Darius III (reigned 336–330 BCE) at the Battle of Gaugamela (in present-day Iraq).

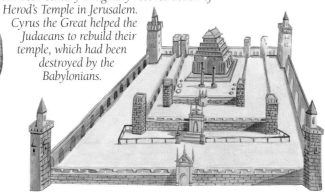

An 18th-century imaginary reconstruction of Herod's Temple in Jerusalem. Cyrus the Great helped the Judaeans to rebuild their temple, which had been destroyed by the Babylonians.

The tomb of Cyrus the Great at Pasargadae, the first royal capital of the Achaemenid kings. After the king's burial in a gold sarcophagus, priests sacrificed a horse at the spot every month.

Tolerance and Order

As their empire expanded, the Persians demanded loyalty and tribute from conquered lands. Once these conditions were met, provinces were allowed to continue with their local ways and customs. After capturing Babylon in 539 BCE, Cyrus the Great decreed that the exiled people of Judah could go back to their homeland. He even returned the gold and silver that had been looted from their temple in Jerusalem.

Who were the Persians?

The Persians were descended from nomadic Indo-European tribes from northeast of the Caspian Sea. They moved south to the Zagros Mountains, where some groups—known to us as the Medes—settled the uplands around 1000 BCE. Others moved on to a region that came to be known as Parsa (the modern Iranian region of Fars), and these people were the first Persians.

Double-headed griffin capital from the city of Persepolis.

Persepolis

Around 515 BCE, Darius I chose Persepolis (the "Persian City") as the site for his new royal capital. He built a palace on a raised terrace, which was reached by a monumental double stairway. The main buildings were columned halls, and these were added to by later Persian kings. The royal court stayed at Persepolis for part of the year, and it acted as a ceremonial symbol of the Persian Empire's power.

Running the Regions

Darius I divided his empire into 20 large provinces, each of which was ruled by a satrap, or provincial governor. The satraps were noblemen who lived in regal style and had great power, but they were always subject to the "King of Kings," who could send orders quickly by royal messenger. The Persian cities were connected by good roads, the most famous of which was the Royal Road from Sardis, in Lydia, to Susa, the administrative capital. The road was more than 1,491 miles (2,400 km) long.

Relief of Darius I from the so-called Treasury at the ceremonial centre of Persepolis.

The ruins at Persepolis. There were once 36 stone columns, 65 feet (20 m) high and crowned with decorated capitals (see left), which supported a flat roof. The hall was probably used for grand formal ceremonies.

THE PERSIAN EMPIRE

Persia, 559 BCE
Conquered 559–550 BCE
Conquered 550–530 BCE
Conquered 530–522 BCE
Conquered 521–486 BCE
Vassal state or tributary region
— Border of Persian Empire, 496 BCE

Reaching Out

Under Cyrus the Great, the Persian Empire stretched all the way to the Mediterranean coast and Lydia (in modern-day Turkey) in the west. Cyrus's son, Cambyses II (reigned 529–522 BCE), won an important battle near the Nile River and went on to capture Memphis and secure rule over Egypt. His successor, Darius I (reigned 522–486 BCE), expanded the empire to its greatest extent, including control of the Indus Valley in the east. At its greatest, the Persian Empire covered much of southwest Asia. The Persians were also pushing into North Africa and southeastern Europe. But Darius I's planned conquest of Greece ultimately failed.

The Persian Empire

Around 550 BCE, Cyrus II, known as Cyrus the Great (c. 590–c. 522 BCE), defeated the king of Media and founded the Persian Empire. Less than 30 years later, it had grown to become the largest empire there had ever been. It was different in style from previous states, too. Persian rulers respected the ways of their new subjects, showing understanding and inspiring loyalty. Their laws were fair. The Persians were also highly organized, dividing their huge territory into provinces that were linked by good roads. This helped with administration, including the collection of taxes from their most distant lands.

Last Great Eastern Empire

The great extent and wealth of the Persian Empire meant that its art and culture were influenced by many different traditions. Persian religious customs had been based on sacrifice and centered on fire, and these developed into a belief in Zoroastrianism. This included belief in an afterlife, where those who had followed the cause of good would be rewarded. This faith was to have a great influence on many later religions. After the failure to include Greece in the empire, Persian rule went into decline. The end of the Achaemenid dynasty and the empire came with a decisive defeat by Alexander the Great, in 331 BCE.

This winged figure represents Ahura Mazda. Zoroastrians believed that their supreme god was in a constant struggle with Ahriman, the destructive force of greed and anger.

A Supreme God

The ancient Persians believed in many gods of nature, including Mithra, the god of light. A prophet named Zoroaster (believed to have lived during the 12th century BCE) began teaching that there was one single god of goodness, truth, and light, called Ahura Mazda, meaning "Wise Lord." Followers of the prophet and worshipers of the single god, called Zoroastrians, spread these beliefs throughout the empire.

A gold daric coin showing an archer representing the Persian king. The coin was named after Darius I, who introduced a standard currency to the empire. Only the royal mint was allowed to produce gold coins.

NEW YEAR CEREMONY

At New Year, which was celebrated at the time of the spring equinox, officials from all over the empire made their way to the ceremonial center at Persepolis. They brought gifts for the king, which represented the tribute for the year that had been demanded by the imperial government. The tributes were presented to the king in his great audience hall.

Conflict with the West

By 500 BCE small Greek island-states along the Anatolian coast had been conquered by the Persians, but the Greeks then rose up against the invaders. Darius I was defeated by the weather in 492 BCE, when his fleet was destroyed in a storm. After the disastrous defeat at Marathon two years later, it was left to Xerxes I to try and conquer Greece. But at the naval Battle of Salamis, in 480 BCE, his 800 galleys were crammed into a narrow strait and outflanked by the smaller Greek fleet.

Delegates from two different provinces climb the ceremonial stairway at Persepolis. Tribute-bearers are also represented on the wall reliefs.

Glazed-brick relief of members of the royal guard, from Susa. The guards were known as the "Immortals," because if one was killed, he was immediately replaced by another.

Art of Many Lands

Just as ambassadors and merchants moved between the different provinces of the empire, so too did artists and craftworkers. This meant that different artistic traditions could continue to flourish. The glazed bricks at Susa and elsewhere were reminiscent of Babylon. Metalwork was also important, and beautiful objects were made in gold and silver

A Persian horseman. The Persian cavalry were greatly feared by the Greeks and other opponents.

A 5th-century silver deer.

Traders of the Desert

The Arabian Peninsula lies to the south of Mesopotamia and the Mediterranean coast, across the Red Sea from Egypt. It is separated from Persia (modern-day Iran) by the Persian Gulf. In ancient times Arabia was inhabited by nomadic tribes of herders. After some groups began to settle, towns grew into city-states and kingdoms, especially in the south. They all thrived by trading incense and spices, which were popular in Egypt and Mesopotamia, and later in the Greek and Roman empires. The difficult journey across the desert became a way of life that created wealth for Arabian traders.

SYMMACHORVM

This Roman ivory plaque shows a priestess sprinkling incense on an altar to Jupiter, king of the gods.

A bronze incense burner decorated with an ibex, about 3rd century BCE, from Marib in Saba (modern-day Yemen).

The Power of Incense

The fragrance of frankincense resin was used for several purposes. The main use was in religious ceremonies, when the resin was burned as incense. Frankincense gives off a strong, sweet smell, which was thought to be divine and pure. The ancient Egyptians used incense in religious rituals and embalming, and the Babylonians also burned it to work out omens from its smoke. Myrrh, the gum of a similar plant, was also used in medicine and perfumes.

A branch of the myrrh tree. Its resin is used to make incense.

The so-called Monastery at Petra, which was probably a royal tomb.

Ships of the Desert

The one-humped dromedary, or Arabian camel, was domesticated by nomadic Arabs by 1500 BCE or perhaps earlier. Camels are the ideal beasts of burden in the desert because they can withstand severe heat and go for many days without water. They can also carry heavy loads.

The Arabian camel stores fat in its single hump, which provides it with energy over a long period.

Arabian Cities

There were several small, independent kingdoms in southern Arabia, including Hadhramaut, Ma'in, Qataban and Saba (see page 40). Each of the kingdoms' capitals — Shabwa, Qarnaw, Timna and Marib — was a thriving walled city that controlled overland trade. At the northern end of the caravan routes, the city of Petra (in modern-day Jordan) was the capital of the Nabataeans. Petra was hewn out of rock and could only be entered through a narrow gorge. Like the southern cities' walls, this offered the city protection against attack.

People of the ancient oasis city of Palmyra (modern-day Tadmor, in Syria) grew rich from their services to traders. Camels and camel-drivers could refresh themselves before carrying on across the desert with their goods. Palmyra came under Roman control around 20 CE.

SEA ROUTES IN THE MIDDLE EAST

Arabian Ports

Sea routes led to major Arabian ports, such as Qani and those of the ancient region of Dhofar (centered on Salalah, in present-day Oman). Spice cargoes were taken north through the Red Sea and the Persian Gulf.

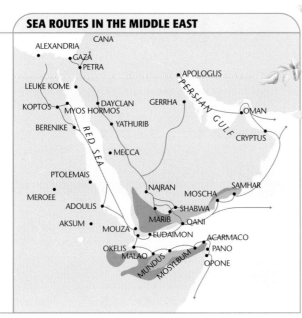

— Incense trade routes
▬ Area of pyrrh production
▬ Area of frankincense production
▬ Area of both myrrh and frankincense production

Map labels: CANA, ALEXANDRIA, GAZA, PETRA, APOLOGUS, LEUKE KOME, PERSIAN GULF, KOPTOS, DAYCLAN, GERRHA, MYOS HORMOS, OMAN, BERENIKE, YATHURIB, CRYPTUS, RED SEA, MECCA, PTOLEMAIS, NAJRAN, MOSCHA, SAMHAR, MEROEE, SHABWA, ADOULIS, MARIB, QANI, AKSUM, MOUZA, EUDAIMON, ACARMACO, OKELIS, PANO, MALAO, MUNDUS, MOSYLBUM, OPONE

A branch of the Boswellia franca tree, from which frankincense (meaning "high-quality incense") is obtained. Harvesters cut into the tree's bark and collect the colorless or pale yellow resin, or gum, which has a spicy fragrance.

The Spice Route

Frankincense and myrrh were produced in great quantity in the southern region of the Arabian Peninsula. Trade routes ran through the desert along the west of the peninsula, past the oasis settlement of Mecca, all the way to Petra and further north. The main land route is sometimes called the "Incense Road". Perfumed oils were also shipped from the west-coast ports of India, and Arabia acted as a stopping and collection point for Egypt and Mesopotamia.

The Promised Land

This Egyptian wall painting from about 1900 BCE shows a nomadic group, possibly Hebrews from Canaan, trading with Egypt. The presence of women and children suggests that they were hoping to settle in Egypt.

About 2000 BCE nomadic Semitic peoples came from the east to the land of Canaan, which included most of modern-day Israel, Jordan, and Syria. Among them, according to the Bible, were the Hebrews. They believed that Canaan had been promised to them by God. After migrating to Egypt, the Hebrews returned to their Promised Land and formed the kingdom of Israel. Throughout their history, the Hebrews were influenced by the great civilizations on their borders—Mesopotamia and Egypt.

Hebrew Origins

According to biblical tradition, the patriarch Abraham lived in the southern Mesopotamian city of Ur some time after 2000 BCE. This was during the Old Babylonian period (see pages 12–13). Abraham's father took his family north to the trading city of Haran (in modern-day Turkey). The Bible says that God then told Abraham to travel on to a new land–Canaan.

Exodus

Famine in Canaan may have driven the Hebrews to Egypt, where they lived peaceably. According to the Bible, an Egyptian pharaoh forced the Hebrews to work as slaves and killed their babies. Moses, a Hebrew boy who was saved by the pharaoh's daughter, led his people out of slavery. He took them back to Canaan, the land that had been promised to Abraham. There is no historical evidence for the Exodus, but it may be that Hebrew groups migrated between Canaan and Egypt.

The route from Egypt to Canaan took Moses and his people across the Sinai Desert. According to the Bible, the journey took 40 years. It was a long, hazardous journey to the Promised Land.

THE TERRITORIES OF THE TWELVE TRIBES

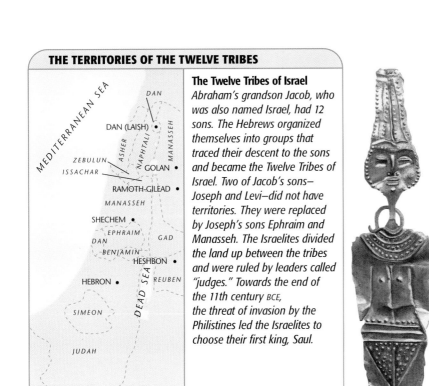

MEDITERRANEAN SEA

DAN

DAN (LAISH)

ASHER · NAPHTALI · MANASSEH

ZEBULUN

ISSACHAR · GOLAN

RAMOTH-GILEAD

MANASSEH

SHECHEM

EPHRAIM

DAN · GAD

BENJAMIN

HESHBON

HEBRON · REUBEN

DEAD SEA

SIMEON

JUDAH

The Twelve Tribes of Israel
Abraham's grandson Jacob, who was also named Israel, had 12 sons. The Hebrews organized themselves into groups that traced their descent to the sons and became the Twelve Tribes of Israel. Two of Jacob's sons—Joseph and Levi—did not have territories. They were replaced by Joseph's sons Ephraim and Manasseh. The Israelites divided the land up between the tribes and were ruled by leaders called "judges." Towards the end of the 11th century BCE, *the threat of invasion by the Philistines led the Israelites to choose their first king, Saul.*

The Israelites were forbidden to worship idols like the golden calf shown here, which Moses destroyed.

Canaanite Religion
The Canaanites worshiped a range of gods. Their chief deity was the creator El (a Semitic word for "god"), who ruled the sky and lived on a sacred mountain. His son Baal (Semitic for "lord" or "owner") was a popular weather god who brought powerful thunderstorms and welcome rain. Canaanites worshiped at hilltop sites known as "high places."

Stele showing Baal, the weather god.

One God
While leading his people to the Promised Land, Moses received the Ten Commandments from God. These began: "I am the Lord, your God, and you must not worship any other god." The Israelites were also told not to make or worship any images or idols. The belief in a single god was quite different from the tradition in ancient Canaan. Moses is considered the founder of the Jewish faith, or Judaism, the religion of the Hebrews.

Molded gold figurine of a Canaanite goddess, dating from the 16th century BCE.

The Kingdom of Israel

THE KINGDOM OF ISRAEL

The Hebrew Kings

Though Saul was the first king of Israel, it was his successor, David, who united the people. David expanded the kingdom's territory through successful wars against neighboring peoples, such as the Moabites. His troops also defeated the Philistines. David made Jerusalem his capital, which was accepted by all the tribes, and had the Ark of the Covenant moved to the city. As well as being an able ruler, David was an excellent musician and poet. According to tradition, he wrote many psalms in the Old Testament.

GREAT SEA
HAMATH
PHOENICIA
ARAM (SYRIA)
TYRE
DAMASCUS
QADESH
GESHUR
ISRAEL
AMMON
JERUSALEM
GAZA
PHILISTIA
HEBRON
JUDAH
MOAB
EDOM

▨ Territory of Judah and Israel
▨ Conquered territory

These stele fragments, inscribed in Aramaic in the 9th century BCE, refer to the King of Israel and the House of David.

Under its first three rulers—Saul, David, and Solomon—the Kingdom of Israel grew in size and power. This was also the case for the new walled capital, Jerusalem, which King David captured from the Jebusites. David succeeded in uniting the Twelve Tribes, and was able to pass on a stable kingdom to his son, Solomon. This allowed the third ruler to devote more energy to enlarging his cities, especially Jerusalem, as well as improving the state's administration. After King Solomon's death, however, the kingdom split in two when the northern region, Israel, refused to recognize Solomon's son Rehoboam as king. The smaller southern region, Judah, became a separate kingdom.

ISRAEL

c. 1020–1006 BCE
Reign of Saul, the first king of the Israelites.

c. 1006–965 BCE
Reign of David, who makes Jerusalem the capital.

c. 965–928 BCE
Reign of Solomon, David's wise son.

928 BCE
The kingdom is divided between Israel (ruled by Jeroboam I) and southern Judah (ruled by Rehoboam, son of Solomon).

The Ark of the Covenant, which was covered with gold and had two cherubs on top. It disappeared before Jerusalem was destroyed by the Babylonians and has never been found.

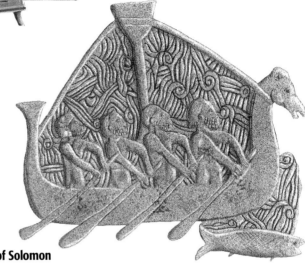

Ark of the Covenant

The Ark was a sacred wooden chest that held the tablets inscribed with the Ten Commandments. The "covenant" referred to the agreement between God and the Israelites based on the commandments. The Israelites carried the chest through the desert on their exodus from Egypt and kept it in a sacred tent called the Tabernacle. After David recaptured the Ark from the Philistines, Solomon eventually placed it in the Temple of Jerusalem.

The Philistines

The Philistines were one of a number of migrating groups known as the Sea Peoples. They came to Canaan from the Aegean region early in the 12th century BCE. The name Palestine, which was later used for their new lands, comes from a word meaning "land of the Philistines." They developed five city-states near the Mediterranean Sea, including Gaza. The Philistines fought many battles with the Israelites, until David finally subdued them.

Wisdom of Solomon

King Solomon is best known for his great wisdom, his reorganization of the state's administration (including the appointment of local governors) and his building works. His most famous achievement was the Temple of Jerusalem, later called the First Temple. Solomon's reputation for wisdom was based on his skill in dealing sensibly with difficult situations. He also encouraged writers and thinkers, and according to tradition composed many proverbs and songs.

A Phoenician ship. Solomon recognized the Phoenicians as great sailors and craftsmen. He made an alliance with Hiram I and invited the Phoenicians to help build the Temple.

Women prepared food and cooked in the busy courtyard, where there was a mill for grinding grain and a clay oven for baking bread. Sheep and goats were raised for meat, milk, and wool.

Cooking and eating utensils: an earthenware pot; bronze pitcher; wooden plate, dish and spoon; and an iron knife.

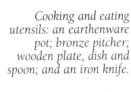

Hebrew Homes

Houses were usually built around a central open courtyard. The walls were made of mud bricks and stones coated with mud plaster. There were often four rooms, including a large living room where the family also slept. On warm nights people used an outside staircase or a wooden ladder to go up to the flat roof to sleep, where there might be a welcome breeze.

The Legend of the Queen of Sheba

The Queen of Sheba and her caravan.

According to the Bible and the Qur'an, the legendary Queen of Sheba made a long journey to visit King Solomon, the third king of ancient Israel. Historians believe that the queen, called Bilqis in Arabic, traveled from Saba (or Sheba) in southwestern Arabia (present-day Yemen). However, no proof of her real existence has ever been found. The legend may have arisen because of the trade between southern Arabia and the Mediterranean lands, especially in valuable aromatics. It may also serve to show the respect that one region had for another.

The Bible Story

According to the *Old Testament* of the Bible, the Queen of Sheba traveled with a large caravan to Jerusalem. Her camels carried spices, large quantities of gold, and precious stones. She tested King Solomon's wisdom with difficult questions, all of which he was able to answer perfectly. The queen was overwhelmed by the king's knowledge, as well as by the wealth of his palace. She gladly presented him with her valuable gifts before returning to her own land.

The Kingdom of Saba

Sabaean civilization may have started as early as the 10th century BCE. A few centuries later, Saba was ruled by kings. There were temples and other monuments at the capital, Marib, and a huge dam was built outside the city. At flood time, the dam diverted water from a wadi into a network of irrigation canals. For centuries the Sabaeans controlled the narrow strait leading into the Red Sea, giving them power over merchant ships. They made alliances and sometimes fought battles with neighboring kingdoms in southern Arabia.

Bronze statue of a man, c. 6th century BCE, from a temple at Marib. The figure may be that of a warrior, who could have carried a spear in one hand and a shield in the other.

Arabian Women

Though it may be that many women's most important roles were as wives and mothers, they also had certain rights regarding property. They could certainly divorce their husbands, and there was a tradition among nomads that if a wife turned the tent around, her husband knew that he was no longer welcome. Women were also able to act as religious officials, and they made popular entertainers at feasts, both singing and playing music.

This clay model from Petra shows two women playing lyres. They flank a man playing a double flute.

Nomadic Tribes

While there were many settlements and kingdoms in southern Arabia, most people in the central and northern regions led a nomadic life. They moved around the edges of desert areas, traveling from one oasis to another in search of food for themselves and pasture for their animals. Inevitably they came into contact with Babylonians, Assyrians, and Persians, who occasionally invaded their desert lands.

This bronze oil lamp from southern Arabia dates from around 450 BCE. A wick would have floated in oil in the basin. The leaping ibex shows that the ancient Arabians were very skilled metalworkers.

Religious Beliefs

The Arabs believed in a range of regional and local deities. Prayers and offerings were made to the gods as requests for the protection of farming land and the provision of a good harvest. Camels, oxen, and sheep were sacrificed, and camel-herders offered some of their herd to the gods by allowing them not to work and to die a natural death.

These glass jars, dating from the 5th century BCE, were used for storing valuable perfumes made from Arabian frankincense and myrrh.

This Sabaean alabaster stele shows a man and his wife beside an incense-altar, presenting offerings to the goddess Shams.

Exile and Occupation

The divided kingdoms of Israel and Judah fought each other, which weakened both. Nevertheless, Israel existed independently for 200 years, until it was conquered by the Assyrians. Judah remained independent for longer, until it too was taken, by the Babylonians. More invaders followed—Persians, Macedonians under Alexander the Great, and the Greek descendants of Alexander's generals. As well as having their lands occupied, Israelites and Judaeans were sent away to other parts of the conquering empires. Toward the end of this period, Jewish beliefs were coming into conflict with Greek customs.

To break through at Lachish, the Assyrians built a large ramp made of stones and wood at the city's main gateway. They then moved siege engines with metal-tipped battering rams up the slope. The defenders did their best to set fire to the wooden rams and covers, but eventually their walls were breached.

Assyrian Sieges

The mighty Assyrians invaded Israel, and in 721 BCE their forces captured the capital of Samaria, after a siege lasting two or three years. Samaria became the capital of an Assyrian province, and many important and wealthy Israelites were sent into exile to various parts of the Assyrian Empire. In 701 BCE, the Assyrians moved south and attacked many of the towns of Judah, laying siege to the walled city of Lachish. The city finally fell, but the walls outside Jerusalem had been poisoned, so the Assyrian army had to withdraw.

THE RETURN FROM EXILE

Babylonian Exile

After Jerusalem surrendered to the Babylonians in 597 BCE, the city's leading citizens were exiled to Babylon. Following a later rebellion and a long siege, the capital of Judah fell again ten years later. This time many more inhabitants were deported to Babylonia. The exile lasted for almost 50 years, during which time the Judaeans were allowed to live by their own customs. At last they were allowed back to rebuild Jerusalem after the Persians captured Babylon (see page 30).

CARCHEMISH • • HARAN
ALEPPO •
HAMATH •
BYBLOS •
SIDON •
TYRE •
DAMASCUS •
SAMARIA •
JERUSALEM •
TADMOR •
ASHUR •
BABYLON • SUSA •
TALABIB • NIPPUR •

Euphrates
Tigris

⬛ Route of the returning exiles

(see page 30)

THE HEBREWS

721 BCE
The Assyrians conquer Israel.

587 BCE
Judah is overrun by the Babylonians; deportation of Judaeans to Babylon.

539 BCE
The Persian king, Cyrus the Great (Cyrus II), allows the exiled people of Judah to return to their homeland after he conquers Babylon.

c. 304 BCE
Macedonian king, Ptolemy I (died c. 284 BCE) rules Palestine.

c. 200 BCE
Seleucid king, Antiochus III (reigned 223–187 BCE), gains control of much of the region.

164 BCE
The people of Judah revolt against the Greek-Syrian king, Antiochis IV (reigned 175–163 BCE), who tried to impose Greek culture. During this revolt, known as the Revolt of the Maccabees, Jerusalem was recaptured by the Judaeans.

Clay figures of warriors on horseback, from the borders of northern Israel and Phoenicia.

This small terra-cotta sculpture, dating from about 300 BCE, shows two women playing the Greek game of knucklebones. This was similar to modern jacks.

Greek Influence

Alexander the Great, who had conquered the Persian Empire, died in Babylon. His generals Ptolemy and Seleucus divided the Middle East between them and founded dynasties: the Ptolemies captured Egypt and the Seleucids ruled Syria and Mesopotamia. Both dynasties of rulers brought Greek culture to Palestine, where rich city-dwellers and others adopted many Greek customs. Nevertheless, the Jews of Palestine were allowed to follow their own religion.

The original menorah was a seven-branched candelabrum that stood in the Temple of Jerusalem. Many later examples have eight branches that are lit during the eight-day festival of Hanukkah.

The Synagogue

The synagogue, or Jewish place of worship, developed as a house of assembly, prayer, and study. The first synagogues may have existed as early as the 3rd century BCE, and they became places where the Torah, or Hebrew Bible, was read and taught. Synagogues became more important as places of worship after the destruction of Herod's Temple of Jerusalem in 70 CE.

Hanukkah

In 168 BCE the Seleucid king, Antiochus IV (reigned 175–163 BCE), tried to force the Jews to adopt Greek beliefs. He had an altar to Zeus set up in the Temple of Jerusalem. This caused a revolt, led by Judah Maccabee (died c. 161 BCE), who with his followers created a Jewish state in Judaea. In 164 BCE they relit the Temple lights, and the Jewish festival of Hanukkah (meaning "dedication") celebrates this event.

Roman Religion

The Romans believed in a wide range of gods and goddesses, headed by Jupiter. Roman religion included ceremonies in which offerings were made and animals were sacrificed. Most Roman families had a shrine to their own household gods. Emperors also encouraged the idea that they themselves were divine, and this became a strong cult, along with those of Isis and Mithras. Jews and Christians had no belief in the Roman gods.

Bronze statue of Fortuna, the Roman goddess of good luck and fertility.

Roman Judaea

R ome took control of Palestine in 63 BCE. The new rulers saw many Jewish people as a threat, especially as they refused to adopt Roman religion. After the execution of Jesus, who was born in Judaea and whose followers believed he had been sent by God as their savior, Christianity spread. The Romans then governed a land with two religions, Judaism and Christianity, which were themselves in conflict.

King Herod the Great

Herod the Great (reigned 37–4 BCE) became governor of Galilee in 47 BCE, and ten years later the Romans made him King of Judaea. He was a loyal supporter and representative of Rome. During his reign he made Jerusalem a great city in the Roman style, rebuilding the Temple and adding palaces, a theatre and an aqueduct. He also built the port of Caesarea and the fortress of Herodium. Herod's parents were both Arabs, which meant he was considered an outsider by many Jews.

Cutaway reconstruction of the Herodium. The circular fortress stood on top of a man-made hill in the desert south of Jerusalem. It had comfortable living quarters around a courtyard, as well as a bathhouse and a garden.

The Founding of Christianity

After being tried by the Romans, Jesus Christ (c. 6 BCE–c. 30 CE), a prophet from Galilee, was judged to be a revolutionary and sentenced to death by crucifixion. According to the Bible, his followers, known as Christians, numbered only about 120 people at the time of his death. These first Christians followed Jewish law as well as the teachings of Jesus Christ, and at first they tried to convert only other Jews rather than gentiles. As this situation gradually changed, however, Christianity became the religion of gentiles and orthodox Jews rejected it.

Two followers of Jesus Christ, Peter (died c. 64 CE) and Paul (c. 10–c. 67 CE), began preaching and spreading Christianity. Paul traveled to many parts of the Mediterranean.

The cross and the fish, two ancient Christian symbols. Since the early Christians refused to worship Roman gods, they were persecuted and often arrested and executed.

JUDAEA UNDER ROMAN CONTROL

The Jewish Revolts

A group of Jews rebelled in 66 CE, after the Roman governor of Judaea tried to rob the Temple treasury. The rebels were led by high-ranking priests, but the revolt was brutally put down by the future emperor Titus, after a long siege of Jerusalem. A second revolt, started in 132 CE, was also defeated by the powerful Roman military machine. According to a 3rd-century historian, it resulted in the deaths of more than half a million Jews.

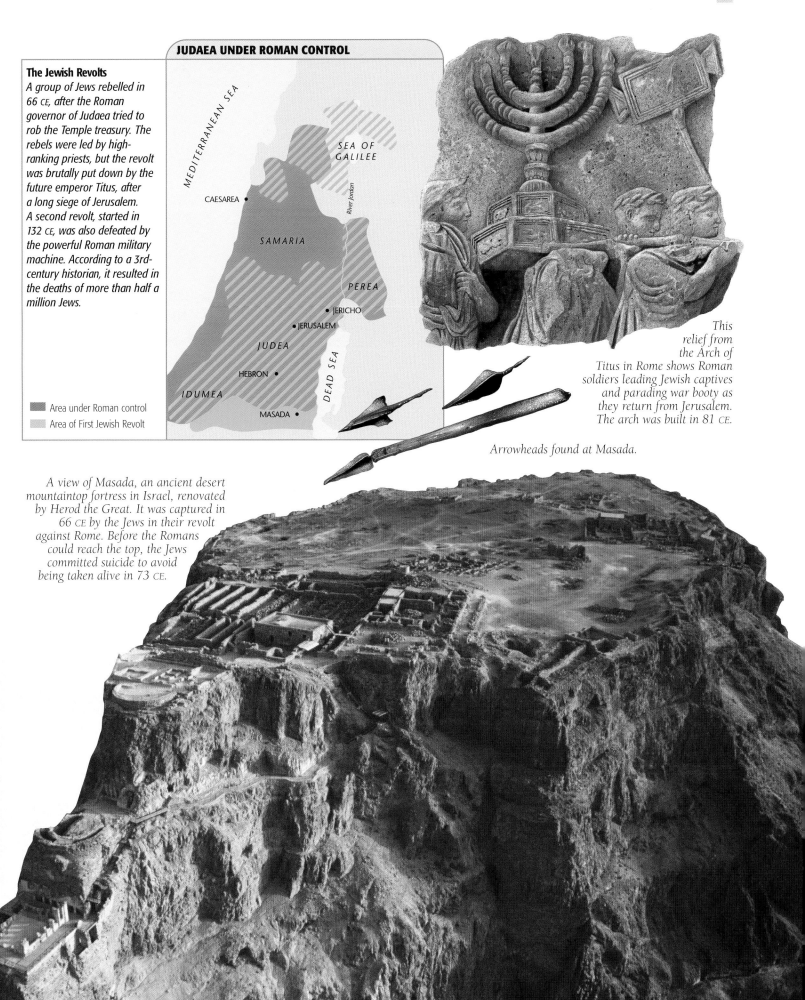

MEDITERRANEAN SEA

SEA OF GALILEE

CAESAREA

River Jordan

SAMARIA

PEREA

• JERICHO

• JERUSALEM

JUDEA

DEAD SEA

HEBRON •

IDUMEA

MASADA •

■ Area under Roman control
▨ Area of First Jewish Revolt

This relief from the Arch of Titus in Rome shows Roman soldiers leading Jewish captives and parading war booty as they return from Jerusalem. The arch was built in 81 CE.

Arrowheads found at Masada.

A view of Masada, an ancient desert mountaintop fortress in Israel, renovated by Herod the Great. It was captured in 66 CE by the Jews in their revolt against Rome. Before the Romans could reach the top, the Jews committed suicide to avoid being taken alive in 73 CE.

Glossary

Alloy A mixture of two or more different metals, usually to make a new or stronger metal. Bronze, which is made by mixing, or alloying, copper and tin, is stronger and easier to work than copper.

Amulet An object or charm that is worn by a person because it is believed to keep away bad luck or evil.

Astronomy The scientific study of the Sun, Moon, and stars and other heavenly bodies.

Auxiliary Term used to describe something or someone that gives assistance or help.

Bellows An instrument used to blow air into a fire to make it burn faster.

Cargo Goods, transported on a ship or other vehicle, which are traded or sold for profit.

Casualty Someone who is injured, captured, or killed in battle.

Colony An area or region controlled and settled by a group of people from a distant country. The Phoenicians founded colonies to make trading with other states easier and also to acquire raw materials, such as metals, and food supply. Some Phoenician colonies were independent city-states.

Crop A plant or its product, such as grain, fruit, or vegetables, grown by farmers.

Dagger A short, sharp knife used as a weapon.

Diviner A person believed to have the ability to tell the future.

Domesticate To tame and bring animals and plants under control so that they can live with and be useful to people.

Dyke A thick wall built to hold back the flow of water.

Dynasty A line of rulers coming from the same family, or a period during which they reign.

Embankment A mound of earth or stone built to hold back the flow of water.

Envoy A messenger sent by a government on a special mission and who acts as a representative of the government or state.

Epic A long poem which tells the story of gods and heroes or the history of a nation or people.

Equinox One of the two days of the year, during spring and fall, when the Sun is directly above the Earth's equator (an imaginary line around the Earth which divides it in half). During the equinox the length of day time and night time are equal.

Exile The condition of having been forced to leave one's homeland.

Griffin A mythological creature with the head and wings of an eagle and the body of a lion.

Hierarchy A classification system in which people or things are given higher and lower rank or importance.

Iron Age The period in human development following the Bronze Age in which people used iron to make weapons and tools. One of the Metal Ages.

Irrigation The process of bringing water to fields.

Kiln An oven used for baking, hardening, or drying materials such as grain, clay, or ceramics (pottery).

Moat A deep wide ditch, usually filled with water, dug around a castle or fortress as protection from outside invasion.

Molten Melted, or in a liquid state under a very high temperature.

Nomadic Term used to describe a member of a tribe who travels from place to place in search of grass for animals. A person who wanders and does not settle down in any particular place.

Omen A message or an event believed to be a sign of a future event.

Ore Rock or earth from which a precious or useful metal can be obtained.

Procession The act of a group of people marching in a formal way for a religious ceremony, a ritual parade.

Province One of many divisions of a state made by a government to have better control over the territory. In the ancient Roman Empire, conquered lands were made into provinces and were ruled by Roman officials and important local people.

Resin Any of the various clear yellowish or brownish solid or thick liquid substances found in plants used to make incense, varnish, inks, or glue.

Scribe In ancient times, a person who wrote down or recorded important events. A person who copied important documents or manuscripts.

Smelting The process of melting down earth (or an ore) in order to separate and extract its metallic parts.

Sphinx A mythological creature, sometimes winged, with the body of a lion and the head of a human.

Stalemate A situation, usually during a battle, when neither side can take further action.

Stele A stone slab or piece of stone, generally carved with an inscription or design.

Treaty An agreement made between two or more states to make peace or settle a dispute. The actual document upon which the agreement is recorded.

Trident A long fork-like weapon with three sharp pointed prongs.

Wadi A river which sometimes runs dry.

Ziggurat An ancient Mesopotamian stepped pyramid-like structure with a temple on top.

Index